AMERICAN TRAVELER

CAPE COD & THE ISLANDS

SMITHMARK

This edition first published in 1992 by SMITHMARK
Publishers Inc., 112 Madison Avenue,
New York, New York 10016

ISBN 0-8317-0509-4

Printed and bound in Spain

To Trisha, who has proven herself to be
a good, little traveler with gladness and love.

Writer: Michael A. Schuman
Design Concept: Lesley Ehlers
Designer: Ann-Louise Lipman
Editor: Sara Colacurto
Production: Valerie Zars
Photo Researcher: Edward Douglas
Assistant Photo Researcher: Robert V. Hale
Editorial Assistant: Carol Raguso

Title page: A blazing orange sunset
provides the backdrop for the Bourne
Bridge over Cape Cod Canal. *Opposite:*
A pair of lonely boats rest on a Cape Cod
tide marsh.

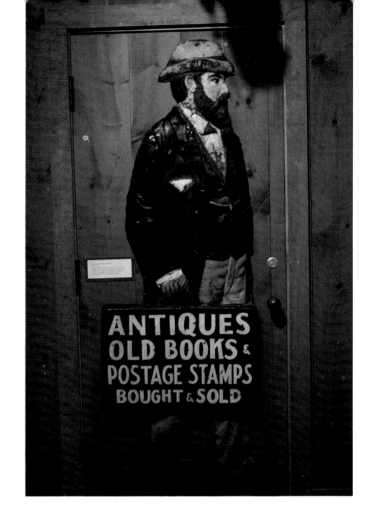

Above, left: Dramatic wooden figureheads can be seen in the collection of Americana known as Heritage Plantation in Sandwich; mounted on the bows of ships during the grand age of sailing, they were thought to bring good luck. *Right:* Trade signs such as this one were commonly used in the nineteenth century to advertise businesses. *Below:* This elaborate carousel, carved in 1912 by Charles I. D. Loof, is restored and running at Heritage Plantation.

Italy might have its boot, but New England has its arm, curled with a bent elbow and a flexed fist jutting into the Atlantic, filled with Colonial commons, antique shops, sand dunes, verdant forests, lighthouses, marshes, and beaches, beaches, beaches. On a map of New England, Cape Cod, Massachusetts, is as prominent as Chatham Light on its protrusive bluff, while in the hearts of leisure-minded travelers, "the Cape" is as inviting as a torrid bowl of clam chowder. Swarms of tourists descend on Cape Cod, and on the islands of Martha's Vineyard and Nantucket, yearly to take advantage of the best efforts of both humans and nature.

However, these visitors form just one thread in the continuous weaving of Cape Cod's history. Native Americans have been here for centuries. Samuel de Champlain, Captain John Smith, and the Pilgrims all came here, followed by the fishermen and millers, Henry David Thoreau, the sea captains, the artists and writers, Guglielmo Marconi, and those who "got sand in their shoes," the people who arrived for the summer and decided never to leave. The late twentieth-century tourist is just one more in the long list of people who have left their marks on the Cape.

Top: Many of the Cape's mill operators were former sailors who adapted their seafaring skills. This pragmatic gray gristmill sits in Sandwich. *Right:* Visitors can examine three-dimensional paintings of Revolutionary War events at the Drummer Boy Museum in Brewster.

Marshes such as this one in Sandwich seem to extend for miles. *Below:* Cranberry harvesting is a common autumn sight in Sandwich. Dry pickers, looking a bit like lawn mowers on wheels, have metal teeth that comb berries from the vines. *Opposite:* Visitors who catch an evening ferry back from one of the islands will be treated to a Woods Hole sunset like this one.

Evidence of Cape Cod's earliest residents is everywhere. The Old Indian Meeting House in Mashpee sits like a squatty sentinel, overlooking the burial grounds where the gravestones bear the epitaph of the Wampanoag Supreme Medicine Man, among others. A bas-relief on Bradford Street in Provincetown at the tip of the Cape commemorates the signing of the Mayflower Compact, while the 255-foot-high Pilgrim Monument nearby, which strong-legged visitors can climb, honors the Pilgrims' first landing. The weathered, gray, pyramidal windmills, in places such as Eastham and Brewster and Nantucket, offer a whimsical Dutch treat to the landscape, and the handsome homes of Yarmouth Port are lasting memorials to the sea captains who resided there. In Provincetown are the artists' and writers' retreats and, near Wellfleet, just feet from where his original complex stood before losing a hopeless battle to erosion and the ceaseless tides, is a reproduction of Marconi's wireless station.

Yet it's the water that lures so many of today's visitors to Cape Cod and the islands. Most are sojourners who care nothing about Marconi or the Pilgrims, but only want a welcoming place in which to soak their weary bones. There are 81 public beaches along the Cape's shores, on Cape Cod Bay and

Top: Standing at the base of the cross, the fisherman on St. Peter's Church at Buzzard's Bay symbolizes the many who worship on Cape Cod. *Left:* Since the seventeenth century Native Americans have gathered in this squatty clapboard meetinghouse in Mashpee. *Opposite:* Away from the congestion of the center of town one can still encounter traditional dockside scenes. These lobster traps and trawlers are in Hyannis.

The naked remnants of a cedar forest starkly stand at Sandy Neck. *Right:* Cape Cod dunes glow in the afternoon sun. They are created by blowing wind following the erosion of topsoil.

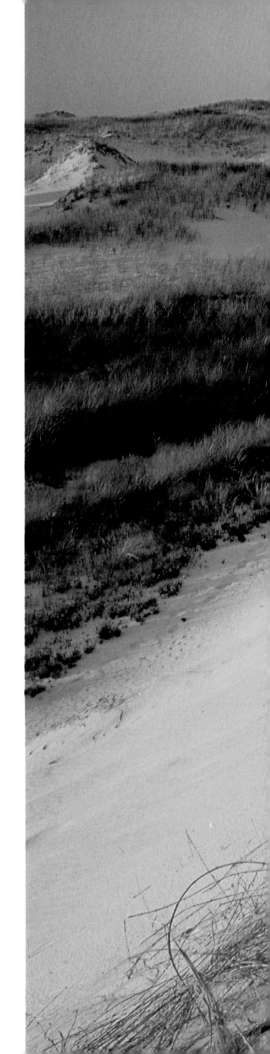

The sky turns blood-red as the sun sets on the rocky shore of Barnstable. *Opposite:* Gravestones dating back a dozen generations can be found in the Dennis Cemetery behind the Dennis Union Church.

Buzzards Bay and Nantucket Sound and the Atlantic Ocean, and on a hot July day, one will find few stretches of sand not covered by the human form.

Many Cape beaches were formed 10,000 years ago, following the end of the Ice Age. After the glaciers retreated, the ceaseless wave action of the ocean gradually wore stones and rocks down to sand. First to live along the shores were the Wampanoags, Native Americans who dwelt in busy communities consisting mostly of wigwams. As late as 1767 there were still 73 occupied wigwams in Mashpee.

The first Europeans to appear are thought by some to have been the Vikings. The story goes that Leif Eriksson's brother, Thorvald, laid anchor around what is now Yarmouth in the eleventh century and was killed by Native Americans while refurbishing his ship.

The first conclusive records show that an English explorer named Bartholomew Gosnold touched shore near Provincetown in 1602. Though today a historical footnote, Gosnold came searching for gold and achieved immortality by conceiving the name Cape Cod. One of Gosnold's crewmen cemented the event in history when he wrote, "Neere this Cape, we came to anchor in

Top: The whitewashed spire of this Brewster church pierces a crisp blue sky. *Left:* With its many welcoming windows facing the town of Harwich Port, the Brooks Free Library not only houses books, but also more than 20 figurines by nineteenth-century American sculptor John Rogers. *Opposite:* Many find spring to be an optimal time for a visit to Cape Cod. Colorful blooming flowers, such as these in front of a Colonial-style church in Harwich, are a major draw.

fifteen fadome, where wee tooke great store of codfish for which we altered the name and called it Cape Cod."

Celebrated French explorer Samuel de Champlain made visits to Cape Cod, as did Captain John Smith of Jamestown fame, who mapped the area in 1614. Though most associate the Pilgrims only with Plymouth, the fact is that these religious separatists anchored off Provincetown about a month prior to their landing at Plymouth in 1620. After some exploration around the areas of present-day Truro and Wellfleet, the Pilgrims decided to sail onward, but not before drafting and signing the Mayflower Compact, a legal document regarded as a cornerstone of American democracy. It claimed that leadership belonged to the majority.

Just 17 years later, the first town on the Cape was founded. In order to alleviate the dearth of space in Plymouth County, 10 men were given permission to purchase and clear land for the settlement of some 60 families. Abundant forests, fish, and salt marshes drew them to present-day Sandwich and in 1639, the town was incorporated. The settlers established a rather spartan community, with rough-hewn huts and a church with a

Preceding page: Majestic Highland Light along the Cape Cod National Seashore was built in 1857. It is one of the most powerful lights on the Atlantic Coast: In clear weather it can be seen from more than 32 miles out at sea. *This page, top to bottom:* The Tale of the Cod is one of many shops in downtown Chatham that offer art, antiques, gifts, and crafts. The center of Chatham has become one of the Cape's most popular shopping districts. Old Glory proudly waves atop a flagpole beside a large gray barn in the town.

Fishing for fun is popular all over the Cape; the Madame B. sails regularly
out of Rock Harbor in Orleans. *Opposite:* Autumn sunlight turns dried
brush a graphic shade of rust on the banks of Boatmeadow River in Orleans.

Ribbons of sand, carved by the fickle wind, mark the vast Nauset Light Beach in Eastham.

Sharp angled roofs like that of the Eastham Historical Society are common on Cape Cod. Built as a schoolhouse in 1869, the historical society building houses a museum where relics used by Native Americans, farmers, and sailors are displayed. *Below, left:* Standing like a squatty mechanical man, the Eastham Windmill, the oldest windmill on Cape Cod, dating from 1793, was once used to grind corn and make salt. *Right:* A symbol of the long-gone age of whaling, the Edward Penniman House was built in 1867 in the French Empire style by a wealthy whaler. It can be reached by walking the Fort Hill Trail of Cape Cod National Seashore. *Overleaf:* Eerie patterns stand out in the tide flats near Eastham.

thatched roof, and, sounding
like twentieth-century tele-
vangelists, were blunt about
their intentions—"to worship God
and make money," they wrote.

Three towns followed in
rapid succession: Barnstable
and Yarmouth, on the Mid-
Cape, and Eastham, stretching
from the Yarmouth border to the
tip of the Cape, were established
soon after Sandwich. In time,
these towns gave birth to the
many others existing today.
Dennis seceded from Yarmouth
in 1793; Bourne divided from
Sandwich in 1884; Brewster
was an outgrowth of Harwich,
incorporating in 1803; and
Eastham eventually split into
eight towns.

Farming was never easy on
Cape Cod, but that didn't stop
early residents from growing
bountiful crops of corn and
beans, using plentiful fish as
fertilizer. Eventually the land
grew less productive and Cape
Codders took advantage of the
ubiquitous waters for their
livelihoods. From the early
1700's until after the Civil War,
fishing was king. Even today,
in places such as Provincetown
and Chatham, fishermen can
be seen unloading their catches
in the late afternoon.

If fishing was the prime
source of Cape Cod's early sea-
related economy, whaling wasn't

Top to bottom: Like an old shoe cast
aside, a boat past its prime rests
alongside a Wellfleet marsh. A timely
visit to Wellfleet might reward one with
the sight of a clam harvest in action.
Just as a fine-tuned car needs mainte-
nance regularly, so does a stalwart
fishing boat; here the Ocean Bird
undergoes a checkup. *Opposite:* Ominous
swirling clouds cast a sinister pall over
Wellfleet's Newcomb Hollow Beach on
the Atlantic Ocean. *Overleaf:* The fleet
is in at Wellfleet Harbor.

far behind. The towns on the Lower Cape were bases for substantial whaling fleets. But Nantucket, by far, led the whaling industry. The 16 lighthouses dotting Cape Cod, from Nobska in Falmouth to Race Point in Provincetown, are ever-present reminders of those who traversed the sea for a living.

A half-dozen or so windmills, relics of another common trade, still dot the Cape. Many millers were former sailors who converted their sail-handling skills to windmill tending. The octagonal mills, standing like squatty mechanical men, were used to grind corn and make salt. As early as 1654 the Dexter Mill in Sandwich was grinding corn, and by the War of 1812 there were more than 400 salt-making facilities on Cape Cod. By mid-century, however, cheap imports of salt killed the local industry.

It was in 1854 that the first train charged into Hyannis, an occasion celebrated with a band concert and a clambake. But the earliest prominent seekers of warm-weather escape didn't come to the Cape until several years later. Distinguished actor Joseph Jefferson built a Victorian mansion in Bourne in 1889, and President Grover Cleveland bought his cottage, Grey Gables, in Buzzards Bay in 1891. Here, the mustachioed president indulged in his favorite hobby of sport fishing for 13 summers.

Top: Quirky angles denote the Wellfleet Methodist Church. *Left:* Gravestones, colored with age, stand in lasting memory in this ancient Wellfleet cemetery.

All Cape towns were connected by paved roads as early as 1922, but it wasn't until after World War II that Cape Cod truly began to prosper as a leisure destination. Sniffing the tasty aroma of easy cash, locals began to rent rooms for extra income. Combined with the increased restlessness and leisure time of post-war Americans, Cape Cod blossomed into the major tourist magnet it is today.

Upwards of 12 million people journey to the Cape annually, most during the heat of summer, and anyone who has ever spent an era waiting to cross the Sagamore or Bourne bridges knows nobody will be lonely here in July or August. Visitation during the three other seasons has steadily increased, too. May baskets hanging outside Falmouth businesses and celebrations such as "Brewster in Bloom" lure tourists every spring. Fall is the quiet season, when travelers arrive to savor the sights of russet leaves and blazing red cranberry bogs and to shop for antiques and crafts without accompanying swarms. And a blazing hearth in winter can stir the romantic soul like no crowded beach can in summer.

The sheer romance of this land has attracted writers and artists ever since Henry David Thoreau first ventured here in 1849. Following the essayist's lead, a full cast of twentieth-century writers and artists have found inspiration on Cape

Top: It was in South Wellfleet in 1903 that Guglielmo Marconi, inventor of the wireless transmitter, made the first two-way transatlantic radio transmission. This bust and a small replica of his station mark the spot. *Right:* Timbers, stone, and sand, sand, sand characterize the Marconi area of Cape Cod National Seashore.

GUGLIELMO MARCONI

THE PIONEER OF WIRELESS
COMMUNICATION
SON OF ITALY
CITIZEN OF THE WORLD

BORN IN BOLOGNA APRIL 25, 1874
DIED IN ROME   JULY 20, 1937

THE HON. EGIDIO ORTONA
AMBASSADOR OF ITALY TO THE U.S.A.
THE HON. JOHN A. VOLPE
AMBASSADOR OF THE U.S.A. TO ITALY
HONORARY CHAIRMAN
FRANCO FAÀ DI BRUNO
CONSUL GENERAL OF ITALY IN BOSTON
CHAIRMAN

Silhouetted against an early evening sky, a solitary surf caster tries his luck off Race Point in Provincetown.

Like a formation of soldiers dressed for inspection, a row of vacation cottages stands mutely in Provincetown. *Below:* The docks of Provincetown have patiently awaited fishing boats through the ages. *Overleaf:* The Cape's odd shape is best viewed from the air. During a summer sunset, the tip of Provincetown looks like the curved edge of a sickle.

Cod. For half of this century, Provincetown stood as the home of the country's preeminent artist colony. Among the writers to work here were Jack Reed, John Dos Passos, and Eugene O'Neill. The Provincetown Art Association, a fixture since 1914, still exists, and many theatrical groups thrive today.

Informally, Cape Cod is divided into three geographical sections. The Upper Cape is the name for what actually appears to be the lower portion, the four towns of Falmouth, Bourne, Mashpee, and Sandwich. The Mid-Cape, made up of Barnstable, Dennis, and Yarmouth, is the hectic area. The region's commercial center is Hyannis, a usually mobbed village in the town of Barnstable and home to the famous Kennedy Compound. Those who want to see the Cape's natural side should head to the Lower Cape, extending from the forearm to the fist. This is the home of Cape Cod National Seashore.

Cape Cod had been settled hundreds of years before the Department of the Interior established the national sea-shore in 1961. So unlike other units of the national park system, especially those in the West, there are stretches of motels, restaurants, and cottages intermixed with preserved land from Nauset

Top: Fishermen head out for a hard day's work off the shores of Cape Cod. *Left:* Color and creativity characterize the symbols many fishermen use to decorate their boats. *Opposite:* In the days when Theodore Roosevelt was president and manned flight was still a novelty, schooner races were a popular pastime. This Provincetown monument honors the winner of a 1907 race sponsored by tea magnate, philanthropist, and sportsman Sir Thomas Lipton.

ROSE DOROTHEA

THIS STONE COMMEMORATES THE
VICTORY OF THE SCHOONER "ROSE
DOROTHEA" CAPTAINED BY MARION
PERRY AND CREW, AT THE OLD HOME
WEEK CELEBRATION IN BOSTON 1907.
THIS CUP GIVEN BY SIR THOMAS
LIPTON FOR THE WINNER OF THIS
RACE CAN BE SEEN IN THE
PROVINCETOWN TOWN HALL

———

THIS STONE ERECTED BY POPULAR
SUBSRIPTION THROUGH THE EFFORTS OF
THE PORTUGUESE AMERICAN CIVIC
LEAGUE.

Above, left: Heritage Museum in Provincetown is housed in the old Center Methodist Church, built in 1861. *Right:* A brightly bedecked town crier spreads the word in front of Provincetown Town Hall. *Below:* Funky little shops along Provincetown's Commercial Street sell everything from toy cats to lingerie to nautical crafts, and in summer they draw people by the masses.

Above, left: The skyline of Provincetown is pierced by the Pilgrim Monument (*background*) and the Universalist Church. *Right:* The epitome of Victoriana in Provincetown is this nineteenth-century cupola, gingerbread frills and all. *Below:* Elaborate and vibrant flora are the hallmarks of many homes and inns along Commercial Street.

The Tisbury Museum, on Martha's Vineyard, is also known as the Old Schoolhouse Museum; it is filled with nautical crafts, art, and treasures brought home by whalers who sailed around the globe. *Below:* Faded wood and a locked door are part of the Mayhew Chapel in West Tisbury, a memorial to Reverend Thomas Mayhew, the British missionary who purchased the island in 1642.

Marsh to Race Point. But leaving the commercial Cape behind is just a matter of turning off Route 6 into the protected wilderness of the national seashore.

Though there are two visitor centers on the national seashore, the outdoors lures, and staying inside for too long becomes difficult. Along the several walking trails are pines and oaks, salt marshes and swamps, and cranberry bogs and dunes. For those who prefer pedal power, miles of blacktop on this relatively low-lying land make for inviting bike trails.

Five national seashore beaches cover the stretch of sand at the ocean's edge, with Nauset Beach being the site of the reproduction of Marconi's wireless station. For a relaxing dip, however, swimmers should think twice, since the icy Atlantic waters are best suited for polar bears. The mildest Cape water generally laps the beaches facing Nantucket Sound, which can warm to 72 degrees on a summer day. The water of Cape Cod Bay, like the Atlantic Ocean that buffets the national seashore beaches, is often 10 degrees colder.

Though some come here to swim, others come to walk, and the most unusual Cape walk may be through the streets of Provincetown. The Key West of the north, this funky montage of art galleries, guest houses,

Top: Stone structures might be common in England's Cotswold Hills but are relatively rare in New England. An exception to the rule is the Old Stone Church on William Street in Vineyard Haven. *Right:* A chunky linden tree finds its own place on a sidewalk in Vineyard Haven.

Above, left to right: A Victorian house that seems to have been taken straight out of Cape May, New Jersey, or San Francisco's Alamo Square is perfectly at home in the community of Oak Bluffs on Martha's Vineyard. The whaling era has left its mark on many spots in this part of New England, including this nineteenth-century home in Oak Bluffs. A diminutive captain stands watch on the porch of still another Oak Bluffs residence. *Below:* Cottages flowing in pastel and gingerbread are the legacy of religious groups who gathered to hold camp meetings in Oak Bluffs in the 1830's.

fishing boats, specialty shops, sidewalk cafes, gay bars, and cozy, narrow streets on the Cape's fist is the most colorful town on Cape Cod.

Yet as "P-town" draws the aware and the eccentric, it has always been a fishing town, though today it attracts more sport than commercial fishermen. The fleet, consisting mainly of Portuguese-American and some longtime Yankee fishermen plying the trade of their ancestors, sets sail in the morning and returns with catches of bluefish, mackerel, and cod when the afternoon sun casts long shadows down Commercial Street.

Perhaps the best-preserved specimen of early New England on Cape Cod is Falmouth. If Universal Studios were building an old Cape Cod back lot, this Upper Cape town would be the model. There's a lazy village green, laid out in 1749, engirded by Colonial and Federal period houses, including the 1810 home of Katharine Lee Bates, the educator and poet who wrote "America the Beautiful." And many a stroller has worn down shoe leather in Falmouth's downtown shopping district.

Stately homes aren't limited to Falmouth. The former abodes of sea captains can be viewed in Barnstable, Yarmouth, and Brewster, as well. The distinguished Cape Cod house, the region's contribution to domestic architecture across the nation, can also be found in abundance. The classic

Top to bottom: Frilly cottages standing like oversized dollhouses line the streets of Oak Bluffs. This group of homes is framed by the posts of a venerable gazebo. A playful cottage could have easily been drawn from the pages of a Grimm's fairy tale.

Cape, a story-and-a-half high, weathered gray from eons of exposure to salt and sun, is best seen along Route 6A from Sandwich to East Orleans and in the villages of Centerville, Osterville, and Cotuit.

The Cape's renowned dunes, on the other hand, are limited to the area around Truro on the Lower Cape. Before the arrival of European settlers, Cape Cod was about 97 percent forest. After the woods were ravaged to build towns, the shallow layer of soil covering the sand eroded and subsequent winds formed the dunes. Until the mid-1980's, visitors were allowed to climb the dunes and it was typical to see children trudging up the slopes, mockingly begging for water. In the name of conservation, however, that practice has been halted.

A few dunes can be found on the offshore island of Martha's Vineyard, but mostly there are narrow streets and stone walls, beaches, fishing boats, and multicolored cliffs. The sister island of Nantucket is partial to scrubby heaths, weathered mansions, cobblestones, and— what else?—more beaches.

The same Bartholomew Gosnold who named Cape Cod also gets credit for the appellation Martha's Vineyard, labeling it in honor of his youngest daughter and the profusion of grapes growing there. The Vineyard was savaged during the American Revolution but

Preceding page: A setting sun appears to rest on the rail of an Oak Bluffs gazebo. *This page, top:* Tall masts, like the legs of spindly egrets, are reflected in the water off Edgartown. *Right:* A bevy of boats dots the water under a late-afternoon Edgartown sky.

thrived after the war as a whaling center. The first real tourists were mid-nineteenth-century pilgrims who came to participate in Methodist camp meetings. They were later joined by Baptists and then by Victorian mainlanders, who were among the first summer vacationers.

Today's visitors come "Down Island"–to the eastern end of the island–to shop in Edgartown or Vineyard Haven, where they can find everything from the latest fashions to obsolete antiques, or ride the Flying Horses Carousel, a fixture in Oak Bluffs since 1876. Those looking for a sample of the pastoral Vineyard of long ago can find it "Up Island," around West Tisbury and Chilmark, and by the lonely, multi-shaded cliffs of Gay Head. Others make waves to the beaches, whether the rollicking foam of the Atlantic Ocean or the calmer waters of the Nantucket or Vineyard sounds.

Nantucket is smaller than Martha's Vineyard and lies farther out to sea; its name comes from the Indian word *nanticut,* meaning "faraway land." Because of its remoteness, the island, which once supplied whale oil to the world, fell into decline for decades after the discovery of petroleum. Thanks to this prolonged downswing, little was built, less was razed, and most of old Nantucket was preserved.

Top: It's all in a day's work for this fisherman off the coast of Martha's Vineyard. *Left:* The tools of the fishing trade are strongly in evidence in the fishing village of Menemsha on the Vineyard.

Grand tall-masted ships are perfectly at home on the glistening waters off Edgartown. *Below:* Some set sail to work while others, like these weekend boaters, take to the sea only for pleasure.

Preceding page: A Victorian Oak Bluffs home sports a coat of shocking pink. *Above, left to right:* A profusion of flowers lines the walk of this cedar-shingled Edgartown establishment. With enough flora to suit anyone's tastes, Martha's Restaurant in Edgartown welcomes hungry visitors. The Victorian Inn is one of many sitting squarely along Edgartown's sidewalks. *Below:* Charming Colonial architecture characterizes Edgartown.

Mystical engravings can be seen on the gravestones in Chilmark Cemetery on the western end of Martha's Vineyard. *Below:* Years of moisture and exposure to the elements have caused the flower on this gravestone to sprout moss on its engraved blossoms. *Opposite:* Multi-shaded clay cliffs meet the frothy ocean at Gay Head, the locale of nature's best efforts on Martha's Vineyard.

Waves and subtle light combine to form eccentric patterns on Nantucket Island. *Left:* Because of its vulnerable setting, Brant Point has seen nearly a dozen lighthouses since the first was built in colonial days. The stubby white lighthouse now occupying the point was constructed in 1901.

Nantucket's brawny docks have greeted many a boat over the years. *Opposite:* High on a hilltop, the Congregational Church overlooks Old North Wharf.

The signposts on Nantucket are hardly the sterile, green, institutional variety found on the mainland. *Below, left:* The Starbuck-Kilvert House is a prime example of an early Nantucket residence. *Right:* Gift seekers will find no shortage of crafts for sale on Nantucket. This shop operates at Old North Wharf. *Opposite:* Nantucket's bumpy cobblestone main street jostles motorists, but is a lure for tourists just the same.

The cobblestone streets and elegant captains' mansions are prime draws of the town of Nantucket, the largest community on the island. The rest of Nantucket is filled with open beaches, moors a traveler would be hard pressed to find outside Scotland, and wild ranges of heaths adorned by roses, cranberries, and bayberries. It is this quietude that most differentiates Nantucket from the up-tempo beat of Martha's Vineyard.

Henry David Thoreau wrote of Cape Cod in the 1850's, "A man may stand there and put all America behind him." Patti Page sang in the 1950's, "If you're fond of sand dunes and salt sea air, quaint little villages here and there, you're sure to fall in love with old Cape Cod." And in the 1990's, visitors still come in droves. Obviously, the allure of Cape Cod and its nearby islands has not diminished over the years.

Top to bottom: Jared Coffin, a wealthy descendant of one of Nantucket's first families, built this stately brick mansion for his wife in 1842. A whale skeleton, ship models, scrimshaw, a lighthouse lens, and blubber-processing equipment are all on display in the Whaling Museum on Broad Street, a mid-nineteenth-century structure originally built as a candle factory. It's rare to find the tree-shaded, brick-lined streets of Nantucket so empty; on summer weekends they are usually filled with vacationers. *Opposite:* Browsing, buying, and walking leisurely through town are some of the favorite activities for vacationers on Nantucket Island.

"Our lady of the Isle" is an appropriate name for Nantucket's small Romanesque-style Catholic church. *Below:* Flowers in full bloom ornament a Nantucket store. *Opposite:* This old mill, built in 1746, contains original wooden machinery that is still operative and used today to grind corn during summer.

The mainland has no monopoly on cranberries. The cranberry harvest is an autumn ritual on Nantucket.

A pathway across the sand leads to the Brant Point Lighthouse. *Overleaf:*
The sun seems to float on the temperate waters off the shores of Nantucket
Island.

Index of Photography

All photographs courtesy of The Image Bank except where indicated *.